a tether tied to space

Epigrams and subversions

John Veen

NON-DUALITY PRESS

For Vickie, Cassandra, Pinky, and Lawrence, in that order.

A TETHER TIED TO SPACE

First English edition published December 2013
by NON-DUALITY PRESS

© John Veen 2013
© Non-Duality Press 2013

Tether assemblage on cover by the author.
John Veen has asserted his rights under the Copyright,
Designs and Patents Act, 1988, to be identified as author of
this work.
All rights reserved
No part of this book may be reproduced or utilized in any
form or by any means, electronic or mechanical, without
prior permission in writing from the Publisher.

ISBN: 978-1-908664-38-9

NON-DUALITY PRESS | PO Box 2228 | Salisbury | SP2 2GZ
United Kingdom

"Just simply say when doubt arises,
Not two."
— Seng Ts'an

"We... in mad trance strike with our spirit's
knife / Invulnerable nothings."
— P. B. Shelley

"Since everything is without substance,
sustain the joke of the absurd."
— Longchenpa

"Luminous mind is the actual
condition of everything."
— Longchenpa

Foreword

Reality is timeless so the question "When?" can never be answered.

If you can't say *when* something arises you can't claim to know *that* it arises. You might speculate that birth and death happen *now*, simultaneously—but timelessness erases even that.

Now thoughts, whether "of" time or timelessness or anything else, have no actual extension in space or time, and therefore no content. We might reflect or meta-reflect on thoughts as objects or containers of objects but that near-process is an extinct, dimensionless memory.

Memories, thoughts and other "karmic burdens" are like flames and water streams: formless forms *apparent* only to the timeless non-form in question.

Reality *is*...?

The epigrams and subversions that follow are a squence of primitive objections to form, most of which also object to their own forms vainly, solipsistically.

They step foolishly into the dream. And while they are not light, they are bathed in it. They thank you for it.

I

Look straight at the seeking itself.
There's your devil. Your teacher.

※

It requires nothing
no belief
no conversion
no breakthrough
no need to bore down
no need to dig deep...

※

See the resistance to *what is* —
to *what is right in front of your face.*
See the inversion, the contraction,
the avoidance,
the rejection of the real
in favor of some phantom ideal.

※

You become aware of your own tendencies
and resistances.

Seeking (seeking answers, seeking comfort...)
is seen or felt as uncomfortable,
even painful, contraction.

Compulsive, instinctive, automatic desires
and fears are exposed.

And the peace of *not* clinging, *not* grasping,
not cowering is somehow exposed.

※

Chronic self-knotting, caught in the act,
is itself the key.
(The key to what? *Who the fuck knows?)*

See the *contraction in action*
without trying to fix it...

Now it's as if there's a microscopic (infinite)
distance between 'you' and 'suffering'.

That distance is healthy detachment.
Simple, accidental renunciation.
Breathable space.

(It's *all* breathable space!)

※

A ghost outside.
Tension inside.
When you look and see nothing's there
tension subsides on its own.

※

The 'yes' hidden in the 'no'...
release masquerading as obstruction.

※

Bodymind contracts, both predator and prey.
Salvation⸮ Love⸮
The breath that comes and goes...

II

Ponder the inconceivable.
Stop!!

※

The presumption of separation
the fear of separation
the desire for non-separation
are all non-separate forms of natural perfection.

※

Separation into discrete problem-units
is barred by reality.

※

Bodymind sense is life-cling-death-fear.
It is immune to facts like emptiness and its own
absence.

%

When the apparent dilemma
(object, dream-tangent...) presents itself
it is *spontaneously* recognized as 'light'.

%

When light rediscovers omnipresent light
it drops the post-threat post-lust tendency
to linger in fear-desire-fight-flight-
hate-love-anger-greed
or any other sticky form of light.

%

If that thing that sits on your chest were real
there would be no in-breath.

%

Moment to moment resistance
is 'divine' pressure,
a tactile hint,
a gift.

The release button was pushed *forever* ago.
Nothing to do!

III

The simplicity of *no-path-no-self*
precedes trying—
trying to understand,
trying to do.

///

Try to get to the point where
the trying stops
when you see the trying.

///

Stop digging
your hands are insane.

///

Why struggle with the struggle?
Look up. Face the world.

※

Free seeing brings free breathing?
What is it that sees? What is it that breathes?

※

Instantaneous: your passage to the next moment
(the next life).
Without you.

※

If you've got time to waste
get into process.
If you've got no time
don't.

※

Timelessness is the briefest therapy.

※

Timeless reality asks one question
when?

※

Surrender is redundant.

※

Inward-turning is another form of
outward-flowing.

※

Every limitation transcends itself
against its will.

※

Nothing has time to gather itself.

IV

Thought-echo
from thought-inception
to thought-recollection
is void
or ask yourself: *When* does it occur?

///

Thought creates continuity, yet thought is
discontinuous.
Thought creates difference, yet thought is
undifferentiated.

///

Thought is not thought.

///

Total freedom: from notions, views, states...
all of which are impossibilities.
Leaving total freedom as the only possibility.

※

Focus creates the illusion of order
yet focus itself is flickering flux.

※

"I know (fill in the blank)" or
"I understand (fill in the blank)"
are absurd phrases implying
a *container* existence.

※

No consciousness *of*.
No awareness *of*.

※

If it's impossible to *have*, is it possible to *lack*?

※

If things (objects, creatures, thoughts) arise,
they arise *now*—*all* things.
But a thing that arises is a movement not a thing
that arises from itself
which means it is never itself
it is different.

The imagined exception to this rule
is frozen in space and time like a skull's grin…
but the skull, too, is alive with change.
Its slow erosion is a cataclysm,
a deafening collapse.
Its erosion is its essence
yet this erosion is never itself.

The point is,
there is only one 'thing' and it is missing!
As such, it is neither container nor contained.
It doesn't arise 'within' or 'from'
and nothing arises within *it*.

The ocean does not contain the ocean.

There is no arising.

(Apologies to Nagarjuna)

//.

Not an idea, philosophy, method,
discipline, or meditation.
Just a gift—an *irrelevant* gift.

//.

It's an implied truth, like absence:
You can't see it but you know it's not there.

//.

Thoughts are thoughtless.
Consciousness is unconscious.
Awareness is unaware.

//.

Nothing to do with significance
just *off-the-chart annihilating beauty*
immediate and weightless...

//.

Notion or revelation?
When the notion dies in front of your eyes
it's revelation.

※

(Leave the thought-valve open
it leaks anyway.)

V

It's your habit to reject *what is*.
Your chronic condition
is a painful state of dissatisfaction
and you *hate* that!

※

Resisting *what is* is natural.
It's what keeps you alive.
Until you're safe.
Then it turns.

※

'Seeking meditation' wants experience.
'Nonseeking meditation'
strangely provides no payoff.
Seek elsewhere.

⁂

The effort to understand
causes non-understanding.
The effort to repress that effort is ignorance.

⁂

Outpacing theory, practice, thinker, doer,
true *praxis* is simultaneous cause and effect,
knower and known.
It alone is victorious.

⁂

The mind can only see "two"
where there is "one"
or "one" where there are "none".

It would capture the undifferentiated
in its differentiating net:
"Here is oneness. See how remarkable it is
compared to twoness."

⁂

You are, of course, stuck.
Nothing can be done about that.
But your stuckness is unstuck.
Nothing can be done about that!

※

The search for psychological comfort,
security, peace
is an ancient, observable compulsion.
It appears to be the reflex of a self,
designed to protect and preserve that self.
But the reflex *is* that so-called self.

※

Bodymind halts at an ancient stop sign
that warns of long-extinct cross traffic.

※

Wracked by obsessions and compulsions;
crippled by doubts, hesitations, fears —
pure gold!

※

Here's that final, unassailable position
you've been wanting,
your bedrock, your fortress:

You are *only* vulnerable.

VI

First attachment is denounced.
Then it's renounced.
Finally it's seen for what it is:
Nothing.

※

That which truly is, is empty, never burdened.
The burden is truly empty.

※

'No action, no actor, no time' means:
No question, no questioner,
no inward-turning mind,
no error.

※

Thoughts and words can't touch it
can't miss it.

The target is everywhere.

Seeking is non-seeking.
Clinging is non-clinging.

Fixed ideas are themselves
as substantial or insubstantial
as space.

What happens when you 'see' this?
Nothing.

What a relief!

※

Complexity: zero.
Proximity: here.
Approximate waiting time: none.

※

That there is no ton of bricks
hits you like a ton of bricks.
The crushing self and its manic picture show
are vapor.

///

Emptiness is the bodymind
of all (apparent) objects.

///

Why bother with notions like
'absence' or 'emptiness'?
It's simpler than that.
Simpler than any notion.

Can you grasp what 'prior to thought' means?
How about 'prior essence'?
Bullshit.

It's quicker than you.

///

The myth of outer objects is benign.
The myth of inner objects is malignant.
The malignancy myth is benign.

///

The aspiring object cannot succeed
born, as it is, expired.

VII

Fear was the tormentor, then the teacher,
then the friend.

The friend... still teaches and torments.

※

When viewed from its edge
— neither heads nor tails —
conditioning is unconditioned.

※

The opening is always there,
it is the painful thing itself.

※

It's blood that inks the pages of your mind
whose words are unprofitably erased
by attention.

※

The apparent shift from objective to subjective
is the shift from "you" to "me"
(two dreams).

※

Take the phrase "I Am That".
Say it.
Consider this:
Every qualifier, *bar none*, is wrong.
Watch what happens.

※

Nonduality pointers
dangle pointy little (tales)—
cut them off!

※

The subject? Always an *object past.*
No interiority.

※

Our 'saving grace'? Grace itself:
impermanence,
the 'self-liberating' nature of reality,
the 'basic space' of phenomena...

※

No religion. No philosophy. *Reality.*

※

Reality: the opposite of serious.

※

Is the spell broken?
(The spell was always a broken thing.)

VIII

Consciousness is a product of the brain...
begs the empirical question:
If B produces C,
what is B doing while C is being?

※

There is no memory of now.
All there is is now.
Therefore there is no memory.

The fear of oblivion
is the fear of obliterated memories—
a cancelled self.
Without memory there is no self.

There is no self.

※

Assertion A: All things are empty,
absent, selfless.
Assertion B: What is asserted in A is
inconceivable, unknowable.

A means things are not things, nullifying the
"conceiver" and "knower" in B
without whom there is no A.

※

(Don't sweat it.
You can't experience your own absence.)

※

When – ZAP! – the open roof
is suddenly your spine's cosmic silo
beware the birth of religion.

※

When consciousness flickers
there's a power drop.
When the tangent is cut
there's a pause that's an abyss.

That gap is called 'infinite void'.
It's the zero in the binary — the womb.

※

Seeing through the illusion only liberates the
illusion.
What remains is as it was.

※

You may find that some illusions
object to the term 'illusion'.

※

Everything happens before it appears.
That's what they meant when they said
"It is written."

But really it is written
after the fact.

They should have said
"You missed it."

///

Two infinities:
All things plus one;
each thing divided by two.

Call them B and S
(really Big, extra Small).

All the way out,
all the way in.

A third: B+S.

(Apologies to Zeno)

///

There's the infinite universe
and then there's everything else.

///

Put the menu down.
Eat.

IX

Unexpectedly, suchness speaks to you
through fear and greed.
Fear and greed are its voice and the message
is: "Look!"

Now turn this message upside-down:
The apparent you, the implied entity,
can *only be* suchness:
"Look!"

※

To the degree that we see ourselves as somehow
freer or clearer than others —
to the degree that we see ourselves as 'selves'
and others as 'others'! —
we are bound, we are unclear.

Yet primal freedom and clarity are degreeless,
exposing all selves and all views as nothing.

※

Either/or vs. *both/and* resolved:
(1) True reality is object- and problem-free;
(2) objective, problem-ridden, lovely-fearful
appearance runs amok;
(3) they are the same.

※

Your friend's delusion is 100 percent your
delusion.

※

You are the playful product of imagination.

To get that backwards is to suffer.

※

The inner voice is the tail not the dog
but the dog isn't the dog either!

※

Stress is your genetic destiny;
continuation its purpose.

You are not your destiny.

⁄⁄⁄

Seek your brains out.
Nothing happens.

⁄⁄⁄

There could not be greater news than this:
apparent suffering has no external cause.

⁄⁄⁄

There's a storm in your head, or there was.
Now the storm's outside.

⁄⁄⁄

When called upon to do so
switch to channel two
until then:
channel one.

///

Dear Illusion:

seeking
is
suffering.

X

That was your last breath
out of sequence.

※

Consolation isn't in the cards for you.
Temporarily OK but not for the long haul.
Therapeutic benefits fade.
Mudra-knuckles turn white.
Salvation grinds.
Serenity splits when you bend over.
Nothing works, not even nothing.
Snap back to the bitch-and-moan:

Welcome home!

※

Agitation and tranquility are identical.
Agreement and disagreement
with this proposition are identical.
Preferring the pleasure of tranquility
over the pain of agitation is natural.
Clinging to pleasure is normal and painful.
Pain and pleasure are identical.
Suffering and non-suffering are identical.
This absurd thesis has only one possible fate:
to be rejected.
It has no value. It points to nothing useful.
Accepting and rejecting it are identical.

※

Not required: insight
Not required: understanding
Not required: order
Not required: resolution
Not required: peace
Not required: happiness
Not required: success
Not required: goodness
Not required: thought
Not required: no-thought

Not required: intelligence
Not required: compassion
Not required: surrender
Not required: meditation
Not required: forgiveness
Not required: trust
Not required: suffering
Not required: non-suffering
Not required: merit...

///

Temperament change is not inevitable.

(Blink past your own disasters.)

///

The 'self' is a bullshit illusion upon which all
proclamations are based.

"Why should I care? That does not *feed* me."
No, it eats you. You should care
that you are being eaten.

///

"I want to trust what you're saying
but who's your teacher?"

"Resistance is my teacher."

///

There's no self in the same way
there's no libido
and no anger and no face in the mirror
and no words.

///

Selflessness is not questioned, it's obvious.
The question is, how can the *fact* of selflessness
help the suffering self?

///

It's not you-against-it, it's
you-against-you.
By stepping into the ring, there's a ring.

What happens when you don't show up?

Any effort toward peace is just stupidity.
Even your bad habits are smarter than that —
they run wild circles
around your phony blankness.

※

Freedom says all needs are wants:

"You don't even *need* life."

※

There's a logic to the impossible,
a vague fraudulence to the possible.
Does the bodymind pause
when faced with the possible
or the impossible?
Death-avoidance is impossible,
your constant habit.
Another impossible habit: to be, to become...

XI

You say, "But no one lives timelessly."
Not true. Everyone does.
"They just don't know it?"
No one knows anything!

※

Thoughts are bitter.
Chew them.
Keep chewing.
They are still bitter.

※

Epitaph:
A sorry fool indeed
spent his life gnawing
on a tether tied to space.

※

"When I'm dead"
said the corpse
"I won't be troubled."

※

The sage, the fanatic, the primitive, the beast —
between fixations *all* breathe the same buddha.

※

Fixations like 'buddha', 'advaita', 'me', 'you'...
are unglued.

※

The sage didn't invent it — he *found* it.
On the ground.
Your ground.

※

Guru waits for you to parrot certain words
and when you do he says "Yes!"
Anti-guru says "Yes! Yes!" without waiting.

※

Your fear coats everything:
How terrified you are of being wrong!

※

Permission...to just *be*, as you are,
in your natural state,
will never come, or if it comes it won't stay.
(What your lord giveth, your lord taketh away.)

※

False guru tricks you and milks your gullibility
claims to be whole saying you are incomplete.

But he's just like you
as whole as you
as incomplete as you.
Kick him in the ass!

True guru *is your sense of incompleteness*
and that's free, constant, never depleted

until death kicks you in the ass!

※

Teacher, your tomes are invisible from space.

※

To the degree that it sends you back for *more*
it's a corrupt teaching.

※

Reject religion, guru, enlightenment.
Reject everything.
Reject all demands, all advice.
Reject this.
Reject rejection.

XII

An infinite number of reasons to seek and suffer,
just one non-reason to stop.

※

Truth was found in a phrase
yet you went on to the next phrase
addicted to release.

Like all addictions,
this one leads to despair.

※

Drink the truth, it spits you out!

※

Compassion is not an action.
It has no origin or focus.

It's another word for 'being'
which is another word for 'nonbeing'.

%

If the sense that something's missing
is missing
there will be no 'spiritual' search.
If the sense that something's missing
is *not* missing
you should know that...nothing's missing!

%

In paradox and contradiction —
how else would the friend arrive?

In this flux, where cause and effect
are everything/nothing,
where separation is the sole experience
of no one,

where particles are waves and waves are space
and space
is dense as a kidney stone...

how else would the friend arrive but as the
ass beneath the sage
in the golden temple
taking a piss⸮

///

When peace is 'found' through words
the supposed causative text is dropped
for the duration:
belief/believer/believed disappear;
we find (we become) our common ground.

When belief/believer/believed return,
peace vanishes:
they (we) are mutually exclusive.

///

Thought, karma:
no time extension
no space dimension
no power
no threat
no life!

※

From a certain view, 'karma' is latency,
predisposition,
tendency, reflex, nature/nurture —
nothing until conditions call it out.

From no view, karma and conditions
are non-separate and selfless.

※

At the gate, turn away.

Turn the gate (the lie) away.

※

Your perfect simplicity is out of reach.

※

Contra-neti, the point...is *this*.
(This place, this moment, this friend, this life...)

※

It's the knot, too.

Afterword

Nisargadatta Maharaj said the point is to *help people get beyond the need for help*, which is very helpful.

Lin Chi said *you are the light you seek*, whether you seek or don't seek.

Shinran Shonin was profoundly grateful for the *always-already unconditional embrace of true reality*.

Longchenpa relayed the story of the Land of Gold where everything—every apparent object, person, emotion, thought, failure, success, wisdom, delusion—is the pure gold of natural perfection. And he said *this* is the Land of Gold.

Both Jiddu Krishnamurti and Seng Ts'an pointed to the smallest moments and said "look there". They looked—and encouraged us to look— straight through all mythologies, all conceptual dilemmas and dichotomies, directly at the present moment without clinging to preferences and *without clinging to non-clinging*.

The Astavakra Gita says something ridiculously simple: "He who considers himself free is free indeed, and he who considers himself bound remains bound."

These teachers and teachings are our friends. They smile and wave to our inner gurus. Somehow we know *exactly* what they are smiling about. They en-*courage* us so that we might en-*courage* others. They share a very personal wisdom, a wisdom that is sometimes called compassion.

This book is an expression of gratitude for all the pain, fear and resistance you've exposed me to, dear friend, teacher, stranger. And the laughter. And the peace.

Visit John Veen's website:
www.nopathnoself.net

Lightning Source UK Ltd.
Milton Keynes UK
UKOW05f1138031213

222286UK00002B/4/P